Don't be stupid.

A call for Christians to believe and live an intelligent faith

Joshua Beck

Printed in the United States of America
First Printing, 2017
ISBN 978-0-692-97711-8

Edited by Samantha Beck

An Intelligo Book
thedbsbook.com

To my wife, Sam.

Brilliant, kind, full of life.

"I believe in Christianity as I believe that the sun has risen: not only because I see it, but because by it I see everything else."

C. S. Lewis

Contents

Introduction

Let me tell you a story…

A story about a guy at a Mexican restaurant

I used to work at a Mexican restaurant.

I know what you're thinking. And I kind of agree with you. A guy as white as I am shouldn't be allowed to work at a restaurant serving chimichangas. But, you know, they hired me.

At the restaurant, between the serving of the chimichangas and the constant requests for more chips and salsa, I got to talk to a wide range of people — all of them very different from me. One of the guys I worked with grew up in the church and came to reject it. We had a conversation about religion and I asked him what he thought. This is what he said:

"Well, until age 16, I was a Christian. After that, I became an atheist… It didn't help that I had a preacher that belittled me for asking questions."

After talking to him for a while, I noticed it seemed odd to him to find a Christian who enjoyed talking about evidence and asking questions. (Since then, I've discovered many people find this odd.) His experience showed him that, for Christians, it was wrong to ask questions. It was wrong to seek out evidence for what you believe.

"You're just supposed to accept it — 'by faith.'"

The problem is, Christianity is not really like that. Christianity is true. Christianity is beautiful. It's a worldview that fits reality. And because of that, there is plenty of evidence for its truth. There are great reasons to believe in it. It's not going to buckle under the weight of your questions.

But that's not the impression we Christians have been giving. We have pastors like my friend told me about, who belittle the curious, the skeptical, the analytically minded. We have Christians who dodge tough questions, using "faith" as a cop-out. And we have a culture turning from the truth and touting tolerance as the ultimate good, leaving Christianity, the

3

bigoted, "one way" philosophy, to fall by the wayside.

Our culture is getting to a point where it has no respect for Christianity. The worldview we hold so dearly — the one we say is the source of our strength, our joy, and our hope — is losing ground, largely because of us.

In a culture where science and empirical evidence is so highly valued, the statement that you should "just have faith" is a gigantic turn-off. And you know what, no wonder the culture is rejecting Christianity.

A worldview that is out of touch with reality is not a worldview that deserves to be adhered to.

We need to show our culture that Christianity does in fact line up with reality. We need to show them what Christianity is. That it is, in fact, worth believing. And not only is it worth believing, but when you come to believe it, your life will be dramatically altered for the better.

I hope to show you how you can, and why you should, do this. My assumption is that you are already a Christian, so my arguments will stem from that notion. (Although, if you are not, feel free to keep reading. I'd love to know what you think.) I'll argue my point from scripture, from the lives of great Christian men who have gone before us, and from my own experience. My hope is that if what I am saying is true, and I think it is, that you will begin, or continue, to do the things I talk about here. It is your job as a Christian to think about what I say, test it against Scripture and reason, then apply what is true and throw out what is false.

Just like any other book you read, this author is imperfect, so I don't claim inerrancy in what I write. But what I do claim is that the principles in what you are about to read have not been written in haste. They

5

have been debated and researched. They have been tested. So please read them in the same way.

My hope is that these words will start a movement of sorts — a change in our culture. A change that will allow the world around us to see Christ for who he is, and not for who his followers are not. It's a lofty goal. And it starts with you.

So read on. Read, and if you agree, put it into practice. Be the Christian our culture needs. Be a Christian who is not stupid.

Part 1:

Intelligent belief

Chapter 1

Why believe intelligently?

"I do not feel obliged to believe that the same God who has endowed us with senses, reason, and intellect has intended us to forgo their use..."

Galileo Galilei

The first step in not being stupid is not having stupid beliefs. As Christians, we truly have an intelligent worldview. We believe in something that makes sense. It fits with reality. But we can't just know this, we must *know* it.

In college, there are a couple different kinds of professors when it comes to giving a test. The first kind tells you exactly what is going to be on the test so you can study properly. The other kind says "Study chapters 1-9. Some of it will be on the test, some of it won't. Just make sure you know it." Now, for the first test, you're able to study everything the professor told you, and you can go into the class confident — knowing that you know the material. After studying for several hours for the second professor's test, you could go in and know the material on the test. But you don't *know* you know it.

In the first scenario, you have confidence. And because you have confidence it helps you perform better. The second scenario gives you no confidence. You may know the material, but you don't *know* that you know it.

The second scenario is the way I grew up. I was in church a couple days after I was born. We went every week — three times a week. I went to Sunday School. I went to church camp. And to be honest, I was a good church kid. I was the "perfect child." In every skit we did, I played Jesus.*

While I believed Christianity was true, I never really knew. I often thought about those who believed

---

* Also, a friend of mine was always Satan. Don't know what that says about him...

differently than me and thought, "How do I know they're not right. They believe just as sincerely as I do. What makes me right and them wrong?" This doubt never caused me to reject my faith. Honestly, I was too invested in church to deny it. But I was holding on to it for the wrong reasons. I was holding on to it because that was all I knew, not because Christianity was actually true.

My youth group had an event my junior year in high school. We called it Fresh Start. One of the sessions was entitled "Defending the Faith." Being an intellectual person (and one who has an inordinate inclination to argue), I decided to attend.

The session was taught by a now good friend of mine. He laid out some arguments for the existence of God, talked about why defending the faith is important, and gave us some resources to look into the ideas further.

That session piqued my interest incredibly. Finally, I had some good evidence to believe what I had believed all along.

Just a little tidbit about me: When I discover a new topic of interest, I go all in. I find and read everything I can on the subject. I think about it constantly... I do it right.

And that's what I did with this "defending the faith" stuff. The event happened on New Year's. The following Spring Break was spent reading. I finished six books that week.

The reason I loved this topic so much was that it satisfied a desire I had had for a very long time. The desire to know what I believed was true. And what that did for me was amazing.

If you *really* believe God is real, it changes the way you interact with him. When you really believe the Bible is the Word of God, you read it differently. And that's what I did. When I realized the Bible is actually true, and there is good reason to believe it, it gave me a desire to read it, to know it, and to live it.

I believe this stuff is important for precisely that reason. Because when a person gets smart about their faith, they tend to really live it.

Imagine that — a world where Christians actually live their faith. Call me crazy, but I think it can happen. And it starts with believing intelligently.

———————

So the first reason we need to believe intelligently is because it gives us confidence, that in turn increases our faith, and our ability and desire to live it out.

The second reason we need to believe intelligently is because it makes it harder to turn away when times get tough.

If a person bases his belief in Christianity on the feelings he has about it, what happens when the feelings go away? If a person bases his belief in Christianity on his ties to the church (like I did), what happens when the church fails him?

But if a person bases his belief in Christianity on the fact that it's true, and has evidence to think so, he'll be able to stick it out when times get tough. He'll be able to rely on the knowledge that he believes something real. C. S. Lewis wrote that faith is "the art of holding on to things your reason has once accepted, in spite of your changing moods."[1]

So not only do we need to believe intelligently in order to help us live out our faith, but to stick it out when things get tough.

———————

Believing intelligently isn't just for us, though. There are a couple other groups that need us to believe intelligently as well. The first one is our own kids. And by "our" I don't mean you the reader and me the writer. I don't know about you, but I don't have kids.

What I mean by "our" is us as the church. The church has children. We have kids going to our Sunday school classes, youth groups, Vacation Bible Schools, and all the other cool stuff church kids do these days.

But statistics show that about 70% of those kids that grow up in church leave by the time they get out of college.[2]

Think about that for a second. *Almost three out of every four of the kids at your church will no longer be Christians after going to college.* That makes me cringe a bit. It makes me a little sick to my stomach. And you want to guess one of the main reasons many of them give for leaving the faith?

They say Christianity is not intellectually satisfying.

We'll cover the reasons I think Christianity *is* intellectually satisfying in a bit. But the point is, if we assume Christianity is true, and there is evidence for it, why don't our kids know about this?

If we want Christianity to be a part of the next generation, we have to show them that it's actually true. We have to have intelligent beliefs because that's something they need. And if they haven't seen it, when they go to college they'll encounter belief systems that sound much more intelligent — and therefore, much more appealing.

So not only do we have to believe intelligently for ourselves, but for the children as well.

(At this point, you've got to be convinced. I threw in the "do it for the children" argument. That always works.)

Well, if you're not already convinced, there are a couple more reasons to have an intelligent faith. The next reason is for everyone else.

"Everyone else" includes people like my friend at the Mexican restaurant. It includes people you meet at work. It includes those angry atheist writers out there. And it includes my kind atheist coworkers. It includes Muslims, Mormons, Hindus and Buddhists. It includes all of those people out there who aren't Christians. All of those people who don't believe in Jesus.

There are many reasons why people reject Jesus. Some of those reasons are emotional. Some are practical, but some are intellectual. There are all kinds of people out there who don't believe in Jesus because they have some sort of intellectual barrier keeping them from it.

For example, my wife works with a guy who goes to a Unitarian Universalist church. We had a conversation with him one afternoon over coffee. We talked for a couple hours about what we believe and why we believe it. My wife and I discovered in the conversation that the main reason he rejects Christianity is this:

He doesn't know how a loving God could send people to Hell.

It's the only major thing that has held him back for all this time. His problem is not that the church doesn't love him enough. He likes church people. He thinks most of them are great. His issue is not them. His issue is intellectual.

It's for people like him that we need to believe intelligently. We need to have an answer for those kinds of questions, because they are keeping people from accepting Christ.

I am not saying that those are the *only* barriers to people accepting Jesus. I'm just saying that there are many people out there who *do* have those barriers. And we need to be prepared to help them.

That's our job as Christians: to help remove the barriers in people's lives so they can encounter Christ. And to do that, we need to believe intelligently.

The last reason is the Bible commands it. That's right, the Bible commands us to have an intelligent faith. First Peter 3:15-16 says:

> But in your hearts revere Christ as Lord. Always be prepared to give an answer to everyone who asks you to give the reason for the hope that you have. But do this with gentleness and respect, keeping a clear conscience, so that those who speak maliciously against your good behavior in Christ may be ashamed of their slander.

"Always be prepared to give an answer to everyone who asks you for the reason for the hope that you have." This is a command to have intelligent belief. You must be ready. That hope that you have — the hope in Jesus — must be well-founded. There must be good reasons for it. And you've got to be ready to give them when somebody asks.

But never forget the last part of the passage — "But do this with gentleness and respect, keeping a clear conscience." One reason people are afraid to be smart about their faith is that often those who are don't behave with gentleness and respect, but arrogance and cynicism. Don't let that happen to you.

Be smart, but be kind. Study God, but worship him as well. Think, but also pray. God

commands worship with both the heart and the mind.

_____

As you can see, believing intelligently is a necessity. It's not an option. We can't go through our lives as Christians and not be smart about our faith.

Not only is it commanded of us, but people need it. We need it, our children need it, and those around us need it.

Chapter 2

What is faith?

"Faith is not what we fall back to when reason isn't available. It's the conviction of what we have reason to believe."

Greg Koukl

Many people think God doesn't want us to have evidence to believe in him. He just wants us to believe. That's what faith is, right? Belief we tag on that covers our lack of evidence.

Richard Dawkins, a famous atheist, debated Christian apologist John Lennox over Dawkins' book, *The God Delusion*. At one point in the debate, this exchange happened:

> Dawkins: We only need to use the word "faith" when there isn't any evidence.

Lennox: No, not at all. I presume you've got faith in your wife — is there any evidence for that?

Dawkins: Yes. Yes, plenty of evidence.

Lennox: Hmmm...[3]

This was a humorous exchange that illustrates the problem well.

Dictionary.com has a few definitions of faith. Here are a couple:

1. confidence or trust in a person or thing

2. belief that is not based on proof

Now, which one is it? Which one is the real definition of faith?

The answer is both. Both are proper uses of the term. That's why the dictionary lists both. Dictionaries base their definitions on a few things. The first is how the word is historically used. The second is the root meaning of the word. And the third is how the word is used in the world at the time. That's why definitions can change. Because the definition is largely based on how it's being used.

But that raises an issue. How do we communicate ideas if we can't agree on what the words mean?

Well, the responsibility lies with us. When communicating our ideas, we have to make it clear the definitions we are using. And when listening to someone, we must make sure we know what they mean before criticizing what they say. That's the respect part of 1 Peter 3:15. We must respect those we are engaging by doing our best to decipher what they mean, and not just what they say.

But the question for the Christian is this: What definition does the Bible use when talking about faith? That is the kind of faith we should have. We should view faith in God however the Bible defines it.

So, which is it? Is it faith like trust — belief with evidence? Or is it belief without evidence?

The Greek word for faith in the New Testament is the word *pistis*. It's derived from the verb *pito*, which means "to be persuaded."

The Greek language had a perfectly good word to refer to a faith without evidence – it was used to refer to Greek gods. And it was never used in the New Testament.

The writer of Hebrews gives us a great definition and application of what faith is in the "faith chapter." Chapter eleven, verse one says that "faith is being sure of what we hope for and certain of what we do not see." Some people like to focus on the "hope for" and "do not see" in that verse, trying to show that faith is not seeing, it's uncertainty. The words I want you to notice are "being sure" and "certain."

Faith is assurance and certainty. This is not the definition many people in our culture claim for Christian faith, but it does fit with the way the word was used in that time — it was "trust," the verb was "to be persuaded."

Also, if you move on a few verses later you'll see an application of this definition. Verse six says this, "And without faith it is impossible to please God, because anyone who comes to him must believe that he exists and that he rewards those who earnestly seek him." So faith consists of two beliefs: that God exists and that he is trustworthy.

Lennox's analogy fits perfectly. Dawkins first has to believe that his wife exists, and then that she is trustworthy. Evidence doesn't take away a faith like that; it adds to it. You aren't going to trust her more if you find out she has lied to you (or that she may not even exist). And you aren't going to trust her less if she shows that she is reliable.

This is exactly how the Bible talks about faith. It is not the wishy-washy faith of uncertainty, but a trust in someone we believe is trustworthy.

God doesn't want you to believe just because you are supposed to; he wants you to believe because you know he exists and he is reliable. He wants you to have evidence. He wants you to *know* he is real.

When we decide to have that kind of faith, when we realize that God wants us to know that he exists and that he is trustworthy, we'll start trusting him. I mean, seriously, doesn't that make sense? Once you realize that your wife is *really* trustworthy you'll begin to trust her more. Why wouldn't we want that?

Once we have faith like that, we will be able to have a much greater impact on our culture. That's the faith our culture is looking for.

They are tired of Christians who don't have reasons for what they believe. And God is probably tired of Christians who don't trust him. A Biblical faith, an intelligent one, solves both problems.

Chapter 3

Is it okay to doubt?

"And this, I think, is one of the most exhilarating experiences in the Christian life: To take a nagging doubt, to pursue it intellectually into the ground, until you have come to a satisfactory answer."

William Lane Craig

The pastor's belittling of my friend was, I'm sure, in part because of what he believed about faith — and about doubt. He believed that to ask a question is to doubt, and to doubt is to not have faith, and to not have faith is bad.

So, question one: Is doubt the opposite of faith?

Question two: Is doubt bad?

I first want to acknowledge my bias. When addressing these questions, I am most definitely going to lean toward the goodness of doubt. I'm going to want it to be okay. The reason, as mentioned before, is that I am a skeptic. It is in my nature to doubt.

But, my bias does not discredit what I am about to say. This particular bias is actually more likely to make me right.

That's one of the benefits of doubt. You are not going to accept something just because someone you look up to said it. You aren't going to accept it just because it popped up in your news feed. You are only going to accept it when you believe it is right.

That is what makes doubt interesting, but also dangerous. Doubt unexplored leads to despair, but doubt addressed leads to discovery. It leads to truth.

27

Doubt doesn't have to be bad, because it doesn't have to stay doubt. As human beings, we want to know what is true. We love mysteries, the who-dunnits, the suspense at the end of the chapter. Because that suspense is our mind in search of truth. The benefit of doubt is that it makes us uncomfortable, pushing us to uncover that truth.

You may notice that I haven't actually answered the questions presented earlier. Well, I was letting them sit there, all suspenseful-like.

We'll address them now.

———————————

So question one: Is doubt the opposite of faith?

(Short answer)

No.

(Long answer)

No. The opposite of faith is unbelief.

Obviously God values faith. It says in Hebrews 11:6 that it is impossible to please him without it. But, even though God values faith, Jesus never rebuked someone for doubting. He did, however, rebuke people for their unbelief.

Doubt is uncertainty, it's having questions. Unbelief, on the other hand, is an active distrust of something.

This is why, in verses like Mark 16:14, where the NIV renders the passage "he rebuked them for their lack of faith and their stubborn refusal to believe those who had seen him after he had risen," other translations, like the ESV write, "he rebuked them for their unbelief." He didn't rebuke them for doubting. He rebuked them because they were stubbornly refusing to believe, even though they had plenty of evidence.

Unbelief is something of which we need to be cured. It won't be solved by an intake of information. The prayer by the father in Mark 9 illustrates this well.

Jesus said his son could be healed, because anything is possible for one who believes. The father responded, "I believe; help my unbelief."

We are a people of distrust. We're cynics. In our culture of cynicism — in my life of cynicism — this is my prayer.

Lord, help my unbelief.

Now on to question two: Is doubt bad?

In the beginning of the Gospel of Luke we see an account of Zechariah. Zechariah was the father of John the Baptist. Before John was born, an angel appeared to Zechariah and told him he would have a son.

For context, you need to know that Zechariah was an old dude. He *and* his wife were. (Well, he was an old dude. His wife was an old woman.)

They were far too old to have children. So in response to this angel of God telling him he would have a son, he doubted. And in response to his doubt, he was made mute. He couldn't talk, at all, until his son was born.

Why would God do this? This obviously means doubt is wrong, because in response to doubt, God shut the guy up.

The problem is that a nearly identical thing happened to another person shortly after, and God didn't punish them.

Who was that person? Well, it was Mary, the mother of Jesus.

She too had an angel appear to her and tell her she would have a son, and she too doubted. But, in a fortunate turn of events on her part, God didn't take away her ability to speak.

Is this simply favoritism? Or is there a legitimate difference between the two? Personally, I believe the latter.

You see, when you look more closely at the account, you see a small, but significant difference.

The angel Gabriel begins his announcement to Zechariah with "Do not be afraid, Zechariah, for your prayer has been heard..."

For Mary, this was completely out of the blue. For Zechariah, he asked for it. His prayer had been heard.

Their responses were slightly different as well. Zechariah says, "How can I know this for sure?" Mary responds with "How will this be?"

Zechariah was punished, not because doubt is somehow evil, but because he distrusted God when he had no reason to. His sin was unbelief. He was a cynic, not in search of truth, but comfort.

This cynicism is reflected in my own life. Many of my questions are based on my comfort in knowing all the details. They are not a genuine search for what is true.

We *can* know God is real, that Jesus is who he said he was. We can know that Christianity is true. But we're never going to know everything. The seeker of truth is fine with a bit of mystery. Not that they want it, but they can trust through it, and they can see the beauty in it.

Mary's request, as opposed to Zechariah's, was a simple request for more information. Yes, there was doubt, but it was a doubt in search of truth.

I told you a little bit ago that doubt isn't always good. It can be dangerous.

Immensely dangerous.

Doubt itself will not lead the Christian astray. If pursued, it will lead you back to Christ.

Doubt, though, is tricky for humans. Because sometimes humans doubt for irrational reasons. We doubt because it doesn't feel right. We doubt because we encounter something difficult in our lives. We doubt because, deep down, we don't want it to be true.

I want to be clear here. Doubt is not sinful, but sin is often the source of doubt.

Therefore, when doubt comes into our lives, the most important thing to do is pinpoint the source. How many times have you fought with your spouse, or a friend, only to discover what you're fighting about isn't what you're fighting about? It's something deeper, more unsettling, more serious and long lasting. Until you discover what that is, the fight will never be resolved.

What makes us think our relationship with God would be any other way? God isn't going to do that with us, but there are always things *we* tuck away in the back of our minds.

Times we believe God wronged us. Times we've done wrong and haven't repented. Those seeds add up, until they grow, and grow, and rear their ugly faces in the form of doubt.

So when you doubt, figure out what the source is. Figure out what it is you're actually angry or confused about. To be honest, when I doubt God, it's most often me doubting myself.

I have moments where I'm unsure if Christianity is true, not because I don't think the evidence is there for the resurrection of Christ, but because I don't see how God would die for a monster like me.

Now that I know that, I look for it when I doubt. I look for the seed of pride and self-hatred, because those are the sources of doubt in my life.

Well, that was a bit heavy...

Some practical tips to help you with doubt. That's what we'll talk about next:

First, find the source.

Why are you doubting? Is it some underlying sin or worry in your life? Or is it purely intellectual? Either way, figure that out first.

Once you do that, write it down. Clarify what problem you are attacking. The simple act of writing it down makes the problem more real, less abstract.

Once you have written the doubt down, go find a friend. If you have no friends, talk to your pastor. If you have no pastor, send me an email. You need someone to help you walk through this. Pursuing doubt should always be done with a team.

Preferably, choose a friend or mentor you trust. Go to someone smarter than you. Go to someone who's made it further down the road of life. Tell them about your doubt, and form a plan to engage it.

Finally, focus on what you can know. Oftentimes the nonessentials of Christianity get us all tripped up, leaving us worried, confused, and flailing on the way down. It shouldn't be that way.

There are things we can know. And there are things we can't.

We may never truly solve the Calvinist/Arminian debate. That's okay.

The topics of focus should be the existence of God, the deity of Christ, the resurrection. We can know those things, and they are the essentials of the Christian faith.

They are important subjects of doubt because if they are not true, Christianity is meaningless. Not only that, but they can be known. They are questions with real answers.

Once you answer those, they can support the pursuit of other doubts.

For example, are you unsure of the goodness of God? Are you wrestling with the problem of evil? Well, if you've established that Christ is who he said he was, and did what the Gospels say he did, then that would be a good place to start. Use that truth as the bedrock of your investigation.

You may still question why God would allow that particular thing to happen in your life, but you can know — really know — the answer is not that he doesn't care. He came to the world, suffered a terrible death, and rose from the grave to save your life, to have a relationship with you.

You may question him. But if you focus on what you know, you won't get tangled up in the mess of uncertainties and unknowables. (I'm not sure if that's a word, but the red squiggly line has not appeared, so I think we're good.)

For someone who has thoughts, doubt is inevitable. We'll all encounter it at some point in our lives — some more than others. And for the Christian, it can not only be good, but an experience that draws us closer to God, and makes us more like him.

Doubt can even be exhilarating. It can be an adventure. Dr. William Lane Craig is a Christian philosopher and theologian. One of the best. In a conversation with Lee Strobel, recorded at an event at Houston Baptist University, he was asked about Christians and doubt. He ended his comments with this statement:

> And this, I think, is one of the most exhilarating experiences in the Christian life:

To take a nagging doubt, to pursue it intellectually into the ground, until you have come to a satisfactory answer. And that will bring a sense of freedom, and victory, and intellectual satisfaction that the average Christian never experiences because he has never taken the time to do it.

So go after those doubts, pursue them, and find answers to them.·

Don't be afraid of your doubts. Go after them.

I'm with Dr. Craig on this one. It will be one of the most satisfying, freeing, and exhilarating experiences in your Christian life.

Chapter 4

What do Christians believe?

"It was by his death that he wished above all else to be remembered. There is then, it is safe to say, no Christianity without the cross. If the cross is not central to our religion, ours is not the religion of Jesus."

John Stott

The crux of Christianity is the Gospel, but it is a religion. Christianity is typically defined as "the religion based on the life and teachings of Jesus." It encompasses many things. It is in part a belief system; it has a set of moral guidelines; it has a holy book. It *is* a religion.

But again, the crux is the Gospel. The Gospel is the heart of the story, and it transcends the religion. The Gospel, the story of Christ, is something more than

41

religion. It's something more personal, more powerful, and much more beautiful. The disconcerting thing is most Christians I encounter don't see this.

Religion, at its heart, is a solution to a problem. Every religion sees a problem in the world — sin, suffering, evil — and offers the religion as a solution to it.

Along with that solution comes a reward for the follower. The follower gets Heaven, Nirvana, a place where everything is at peace. All suffering is gone.

The message of religion is that with obedience comes a reward. With obedience comes a life that you've always wanted. And that sounds great. I know I would love to be set free from the suffering of this world.

That's not bad. I think there is truth to that message. We all long for something more than this life. Every religion contains some version of that same storyline because some version of that exists. We long for it because it's there.

But religion and the Gospel are different.

Religion is the pursuit of a place. The Gospel is the pursuit of a person.

Religion says obedience, therefore Heaven. The Gospel says Jesus, therefore Jesus. The point of eternal life is to be with Christ. We're not in it to get to Heaven; we're in it to get to him.

As I mentioned, every religion is the solution to a problem. We learn at the very beginning of the Bible what the problem is. If you ask a random person at your church what the Bible says the problem is, they'll probably say the problem is that man sinned. While that's basically the right answer, it misses the point. The reason why sin is such a terrible thing is that it separates us from God. The real problem is not that we sinned, the problem is that we're separated —

43

we're separated from our Creator and the relationship needs restored.

Jesus, then, came as a man and lived a sinless life. He lived a life in perfect relationship with God. That status gave him the ability to be a sacrifice for us.

The problem is that God is perfect. As a perfect being, he can't coexist with sin. His very nature prohibits a relationship with a being in sin. So, our sin means we can't be in relationship with him.

The relationship is broken because of the barrier of sin. Sin needs to be wiped away. We need to be cleansed.

Many people will ask, Why can't God just forgive our sins? What's the point in him being sacrificed? In *The Reason for God*, Timothy Keller answers this question by giving an analogy. He writes,

> Imagine that someone borrows your car, and as he backs it out of the driveway he strikes a gate, knocking it down along with part of the wall. Your property insurance doesn't cover the gate and the

garden wall. What can you do? There are essentially two options. The first is to demand that he pay for the damages. The second is to refuse to let him pay anything. There may also be middle-of-the-road solutions in which you both share the payment. Notice that in every option the cost of the damage must be borne by *someone*. Either you or he absorbs the cost for the deed, but the debt does not somehow vanish into thin air. Forgiveness, in this illustration, means bearing the cost for his misdeed yourself.⁵

John 3:16 contrasts death with everlasting life. It says that the result of following Christ is life, the result of not following him is death. This is because God *is* life. Without him life can't exist.

I saw a tweet from an atheist asking what would happen to the world if God were to cease to exist. He assumed the answer was that the world would keep on going the way it was — no one would notice anything. His point was that anyone would answer this way, because God isn't actually doing anything in the world. But according to the Bible, if God were to cease to exist the world would cease to exist as well. Everything is held together by him.

The punishment for sin is death. Not because God thought it was the most brutal thing he could threaten us with, but because death is the natural result of being separated from God. It's not so much a punishment as it is a natural byproduct.

So, going with the Keller illustration: The debt is death, and it must be paid. God can't just ignore it, because something has been broken and someone must cover the cost. That's why Jesus died. He, not having broken anything himself, offered himself as a sacrifice for us. He chose to cover the cost. He took our sin upon him, and the natural result was that he died. He died the death of humanity.

————————

Christianity isn't about getting Heaven, it's about getting God. When you realize this, it changes the way you live your life.

I used to live like the former were true. I went to church because that's what I was supposed to do. I read the Bible occasionally, but only because it's what I was told to do. But I knew that if I didn't read it every day I wouldn't be banned from Heaven, so I didn't. I did the things I was supposed to do, because I wanted to get to Heaven, I wanted to be "saved". But I didn't do any more because I didn't have a real reason. Why go above and beyond if you get the same result?

When you realize Heaven is not the point — when you realize "being saved" is not the end goal — you begin to live differently. If the goal is Christ and not Heaven, you go to church because being in a community of believers is the best way to draw closer to him. If the goal is Christ, then you read the Bible because it helps you know him better.

Christianity then, is not simply a religion. Christianity is the Gospel. The Gospel *results* in a set of beliefs. And these beliefs, as mentioned in an earlier chapter, you must be able to explain and defend. The Gospel *results* in a set of moral guidelines, but those guidelines are not to be obeyed to gain salvation, they are obeyed because you can't help but please the God you love.

C. S. Lewis wrote a trilogy of science fiction novels. They're typically referred to as "the space trilogy," because they take place on other planets. The second book in the trilogy is called *Perelandra*. Perelandra is the planet we call Venus. The main character in this book, and the trilogy as a whole, is a man named Elwin Ransom. He is a scholar, a philologist, but has gotten wrapped up in a slew of events that has resulted in him being sent on a mission to Perelandra. He is sent by Oyarsa, the angelic ruler of Mars — the destination of the first novel.

Once he is there, he discovers this planet is inhabited by human-like people as well, but there are only two of them. There are plants, and mountains, and animals, but only two humans. The planet is a paradise of sorts. He soon realizes this planet's civilization is very young. So young that they have not yet fallen into sin. The two human-like beings he finds are their "Adam and Eve." The female's name is Tinidril.

The problem is that a man named Weston, the antagonist in the first story, possessed by Satan, shows up and tries to tempt Tinidril to sin. He attempts to persuade her to disobey the one command she had set before her, just like Adam and Eve. This goes on for days, and Ransom does whatever he can to stop this from happening.

The Unman (Weston possessed by Satan), continues to tempt Tinidril, and Ransom continues to argue the other side. Finally, Ransom realizes the only way to end this is to physically attack the Unman. He worries, though, what might happen. Ransom is a scholar, never having been in a fight. The Unman is much larger than him and, being possessed by Satan, has no restraint.

Maleldil (God) casts the Unman, Tinidril, and even the nearby animals, into a deep sleep. During this time, Ransom has a conversation with Maleldil. Maleldil tells Ransom "This can't go on."

This scene is much like the scene of Jesus in the Garden of Gethsemane before heading to the cross. No one else is there, just him and God. And just like Jesus, Ransom pleas to be pardoned from the act, knowing that it will bring excruciating pain.

Maleldil then said, "It is not for nothing that you are named Ransom."

Ransom realizes this one event is what he was predestined to do. He was born in order to save the world of Perelandra from the evil and suffering we encounter on Earth.

His only comfort came when Maleldil tells him, "My name is also Ransom."

Lewis writes, "He whom the other worlds call Maleldil, was [our] world's ransom, his own ransom..."[6]

The story of the Gospel, of Christianity, is a beautiful one. It's a story of love and pain. It's a story of a hero who comes and saves the day. It's all the great stories we've ever loved, all wrapped up in one *true* story.

It's the story of a God who loves so much that he offers himself as a sacrifice so we can be in relationship with him. Through this, and only this, we have hope. If we choose to follow Christ, to make him our decision maker, our leader — then we will have him. And because we have him, we have life.

Jimmy Needham is one of my favorite singer-songwriters. He wrote this in his song called *Forgiven and Loved,*

51

O I tried and tried to rectify
my hopeless situation
But I bought the lie I still have work to do
Now I'm working nine to five like I can earn
my own salvation
But there is no condemnation in You

Oh He died, He died, to rectify
my hopeless situation
And His blood commands my guilt to leave
Now on Calvary I stand
Empty pockets, open hands
Oh there is no condemnation for me

Chapter 5

Is Christianity true?

"I believe in Christianity as I believe that the sun has risen: not only because I see it, but because by it I see everything else."

C. S. Lewis

Now that we know what Christianity is, let's see if it's actually true.

We know something is true by looking at the evidence for it. We look at what the claim is, then investigate it to see if lines up with reality.

You do this every day. If your child tells you they've cleaned their room, to know for sure if their statement is true, you go to the room. You look at the evidence and see if the statement matches reality.

The crux of Christianity is that Jesus died and rose again. He came, lived a perfect life, and sacrificed himself for our sins. So, to know if Christianity is true, we need to look at the claim of Jesus. We need to take a look and see if that statement, that Jesus died and rose again, lines up with reality. If it does, Christianity is true. If it doesn't, Christianity is not true.

It all hangs on this truth. The Apostle Paul wrote this in 1 Corinthians 15:14-19:

> And if Christ has not been raised, then our preaching is in vain and your faith is in vain. We are even found to be misrepresenting God, because we testified about God that he raised Christ, whom he did not raise if it is true that the dead are not raised. For if the dead are not raised, not even Christ has been raised. And if Christ has not been raised, your faith is futile and you are still in your sins. Then those also who have fallen asleep in Christ have perished. If in Christ we have hope in this life only, we are of all people most to be pitied.

"If Christ has not been raised, your faith is futile and you are still in your sins." Christianity rests on the claim that Jesus died and rose again. If this claim is not true, Christianity crumbles.

Now, I could take a lot of different approaches to show you that Jesus died and rose again, and therefore Christianity is true. I could cover C. S. Lewis' Trilemma. I could go for Habermas' minimal facts approach. I could rehash what has been written by many different amazing scholars like William Lane Craig, Mike Licona, N.T. Wright, Alvin Plantinga, and Lee Strobel. But to be honest, it just wouldn't be that great, because it's not from me. I'm an amateur. They're the pros.

So what I'll do is direct you to those scholars, who you can find on the resources page at thedbsbook.com, and tell you about the aspect of Christianity I find most convincing.

———————————

C. S. Lewis wrote, "I believe in Christianity as I believe that the sun has risen; not only because I see it, but because by it, I see everything else."[8]

I agree. I believe in Christianity because there is evidence for it. There are all kinds of things I could point out to argue for its truth. Like the sun, I can see it. But I also believe in Christianity because it allows me to see the world much more clearly.

Christianity is like a set of glasses, and we are legally blind. Without it, we can't see the world very well. There are all kinds of things that just don't make sense. But when I put on the lens of Christianity, things come into focus. That doesn't mean I don't still have questions. But I've discovered that Christianity makes sense of the world around me in a way that no other worldview does.

What I'm going to tell you about next is a fantastic example of this. And this example is a major part of why I believe in Christianity. It's not a knock-out argument. I would never claim that it is. There's rarely a knock-out argument for anything. The apparent silver bullets often turn out to be Nerf. And while Nerf bullets are fun, claiming they can kill makes you sound more like a car salesman than a scholar.

What I claim for this is much more modest. I believe this is a clue. A clue to the truth of the Christian message. It doesn't prove Christianity. But it has shown me that, as opposed to any other religion, it makes sense. This clue has played a major role in my life. It's what has formed the tipping point for me. So it's what I'm going to write to you about. For more, again, please check out the resources. You'll find more scholarly and comprehensive approaches there. My goal here, as Greg Koukl says, is simply to put a stone in your shoe.

Grace.

Grace is the crux of the Christian message. Ephesians 2:8 says, "For it is by grace you have been saved, through faith—and this is not from yourselves, it is the gift of God."

Salvation comes by grace. The grace of the cross. Jesus lived a perfect life and gave himself as a sacrifice for us all. And even though you've heard that statement countless times in your life (so many that its meaning is probably lost on you) take a second and contemplate it.

It's an amazing truth.

This method of salvation is so entirely practical it's crazy. And the practicality of Christian salvation, I believe, is one of the greatest evidences of its truth.

Think about it. All the other religions in the world require you to do certain things to gain salvation. You have to accomplish sinlessness on your own. The god, or gods, tell you what you are supposed to do, but it is your responsibility to carry it out. Once you accomplish this, you gain eternal life.

But is that really practical? Does it really work?

Look at the Pharisees in the New Testament. Outwardly, they were really good at not sinning. But because of that, they were inwardly prideful. They couldn't actually become free from sin, because by accomplishing the feat of abstaining from outward sins, they fell prey to the inward sin of self-righteousness.

They earned it. And the person next to them didn't. They were really good at self-control. But self-control, without grace, leads to pride.

I've seen this in my own life.

Since I was a kid I was always considered the perfect one. The one who never did anything wrong — the goodie-two-shoes, if you will. I took hold of that identity and ran with it. I expected myself to be perfect, and even though I wouldn't show it, I expected that from other people as well. When I was doing pretty well I looked at others and felt smug. I was the good one, the spiritual one.

But when I didn't measure up, (which was most of the time) I felt endlessly guilty. I would fret over it constantly. I thought about stupid things I did for weeks on end. And every once in a while, I would remember something from a few months before, and a warm surge of shame would take me over again.

This back and forth between feeling like I was good because of what I did or didn't do, to feeling awful for what I did or didn't do, is a roller coaster I'm still trying to recover from.

The two extremes I have seen in my own life — the prideful Pharisee and the shame-filled sinner — are a result of a works-based religion. It's the result of the belief that I earn my salvation — that my relationship with God is based on what I do.

And this system is how nearly every religion works. Buddhism requires you to get to a point where you have no desires, at that time you reach enlightenment. But that state is achieved by you. Mormonism says salvation comes by works *and* by grace, not just grace.

Islam says salvation comes by works, and you can never really know if you have done enough to earn it.

My wife works with a Muslim woman, one who has been Muslim all her life. They had a conversation about what she believes about salvation. She said straight up that in the end, Allah will weigh your good works against your bad works and whichever wins out determines your eternity.

All other religions have this component. They require you to do something to gain salvation.

Even though I would say that I didn't believe in that structure, the way I lived betrayed the fact that I actually did. And, again, the result is the pride and shame I felt.

Christianity, on the other hand, provides a religion where the receiver of salvation doesn't earn it on their own. They can't. Salvation is supplied by God. It's a gift. One that can't be earned.

By receiving salvation this way, the receivers can't become prideful. They had nothing to do with it.

And not only can they not become prideful, but they become more valuable. This salvation was given to them, and it didn't have to be. It was given to them by the Creator. The one upon whom the standard of morality they have failed to meet is based. The fact that the God of the universe values them enough to give them this remarkable gift — and the fact that it cost him so much to give — brings enormous worth to the individual.

So we see that Christianity provides a remarkable balance that cannot be achieved by any other religion. You can't become prideful, because you didn't do it on your own. And you can't be depreciated, because you are valuable enough to be given the gift.

Discovering this in my own life has had huge implications. I can't be prideful. I can't look down on others because of the lack of goodness in their lives, because I'm not the reason for the goodness in mine.

And not only can I not have pride, but I also can't feel shame. Because the God of the universe loves me. He gave himself up for me. He took my punishment, so I don't have to.

This truth of grace is like Goldilocks' porridge. It doesn't bloat you with pride and it doesn't haunt you with shame. It's just right.

When you look deep down inside yourself, I think you'll find you desire something like this. You know the pride and the shame you feel. And you want something that can take it away.

I can't help but wonder why we would all have this desire if there wasn't something that could satisfy it. And grace is so exquisitely practical and unbelievably beautiful I don't see how it couldn't be true.

While this is not a silver bullet, it suggests the truth of the Christian message. I encourage you to check out some of the resources in the guide to get some more in-depth, and academic, arguments for the truth of Christianity. I think you'll be surprised at the amount of evidence you find. I know I was.

Part 2:
Intelligent living

Chapter 6

Why live intelligently?

"Surely the principles of Christianity lead to action as well as meditation."

William Pitt

I went to bed last night later than I wanted to. It was an innocent mistake.

I was scheduling my next few weeks when I should have been writing a paper. I often schedule in order to *feel* productive, while not actually *being* productive.

Also, I watch Netflix. Sam and I have been watching *Friends*. The arrival of *Friends* on Netflix is like the arrival of friends in real life — it's enjoyable, but the concept of time ceases to exist.

Anyway. I went to bed later than I should have, after not doing what I should have been doing.

66

Then this morning my alarm went off. And, like most days, I hit the snooze button. Only this time I apparently didn't hit the snooze button... I turned the alarm off. This resulted in (again, like most days) a rush to get ready and a just-in-time arrival to class.

Days like this are not what life should be like. They're not what I want life to be like. But, as you probably know, days like this are what most of our lives are made of.

The thing is, they don't have to be.

My best days are the ones when I wake up *not* hitting the snooze button. I have time to get ready, read, write, and get to class or work on time. On days that start that way I am much more calm. I get much more done. I stick to my plans. And days like that are the days I actually do something that matters.

There's rarely a day that begins in rush and ends with meaning. But days that start meaningfully tend to end meaningfully.

What causes me, and I'm sure many other people, to live our lives like this is simply that we're not thinking it through. We're not being intentional. We're just living our lives, like we always have, and like we always will.

We wake up in the same way every day, take the same route to work, the same route home, eat the same kinds of meals, live the same kinds of lives. We don't really think about how we're doing things. We just do them. And this is exactly what I want to challenge you to *not* do.

Don't just live your life. Think about the way you live your life. Live it in a way that makes sense. Be intentional about it. When you are intentional about the way you live, your life will have much more meaning.

———————————

Have you ever asked yourself questions like:

If I change the way I start my day, how will it affect the rest of my day? Is the way I'm doing my work the most effective way to do it? How are the other people in my field doing things? How are they different? Are they doing it better? If so, why are they better? How is my relationship with my spouse? Why is it the way it is? What could I change in our relationship to make it better?

Thinking about your life is important because your life won't get better unless you make it better. And you can't make it better unless you know why it is the way it is. Without knowledge, growth can't happen.

It matters that we live our lives intentionally because our lives matter. Once this life is over, we won't have another chance to affect the people on Earth.

While we're here, God wants us to make the most of it. Ephesians 5:16 tells us to "make the best use of the time, because the days are evil." Ephesians 2:10 says, "For we are his workmanship, created in Christ Jesus for good works, which God prepared beforehand, that we should walk in them."

The narrative of the Bible as a whole assumes that we are here for a purpose. Why would God create us and just want us to live without making a difference? Why would he create us to live a life simply for the purpose of living?

He didn't. He wants us to do something. He wants us to use the gifts he has given us to do something that matters in this world. Our job is to be like him, and he is not idle. He is an active creator, bringing goodness, beauty, truth, and love into the world. We are to do the same.

If we are purposeful with our lives, we will create and do more. Not only that, but what we create and do will be better than before.

Christians, as believers in the Creator of the universe, should be creators themselves. In the introduction to the Gospel of John, the apostle begins by writing, "In the beginning was the Word, and the Word was with

God, and the Word was God. The same was in the beginning with God. All things were made by him; and without him was not any thing made that was made. In him was life; and the life was the light of men."

The Word, being Christ, was there in the beginning. "All things were made by him." He is a creator. He is the source of the beauty we see in the world. He thought up the beauty that is the majestic, white-tipped mountains, the billowing, blue sea, and the unrivaled elegance of the human body.

I don't know if you noticed, but even the displays of humanity's most advanced creation, the computer, often wear the beauty of the creator's work.

For the past eight years, the default wallpaper on the Mac operating system has been some sort of image from nature. Whether it was a picture of the solar system, of the ocean, or of a mountain, they were all from nature. And the same goes for the iPhone and iPad operating system.

God has implanted in us a desire for beautiful creation, and he is the ultimate creator. As believers in that kind of God, it is our job to emulate him. It is our job to pursue that desire implanted in us and create like he does. He wants us to make great things. It is a tragic failure on the part of modern Christianity that we are not known for beautiful creation.

We should be known for our great art, for our beautiful music, for our delightful movies, and for our innovative businesses. But we're not.

The solution, in part, is to be smart. To think about the way we live our lives. To realize the Christian worldview has something to say about life, and we need to know what it is. Once we commit to live our lives intelligently, we'll start to make a difference in our world.

We'll reach people, not only because our message is true, but because it's beautiful.

Chapter 7

How does your worldview affect your work?

"The place God calls you to is where your deep gladness and the world's deep hunger meet."

Frederick Buechner

You could say that work is bringing order to chaos. The receptionist makes order out of clients. The carpenter takes wood and brings it form. The programmer makes pixels move into their proper place.

We all spend our time bringing form to the formless. (See where I'm going here?)

God's first act was to do just that. God created. Genesis 1:2 says, "the earth was formless and void, darkness was over the face of the deep," then God said, "Let there be light." And on and on, until "it was good."

73

God's first act was an act of work.

Then in verses 26-28, we hear about God's plan for humanity. In verse 26 God says, "Let us make man in our image, after our likeness."

There's a lot of talk over this concept — What does it mean to be made in the image of God?

There are all kinds of answers to this question. Some say we have important traits like God has, that other animals don't, and those traits make up the image of God in us. Things like reason, language, and a moral compass.

Much like the rest of Scripture, (and every other book) it's important to look at the context — including the culture the book was written in. In the time Genesis was written, there was a very specific idea that was meant when speaking of "the image of" something.

In the Ancient Near East, the cities were built around particular religions. The center of every city included a temple, where their particular god would be worshipped. And in the cities, kings and queens would establish themselves by claiming to be representatives of their deities. The kings and queens became known as the "images of" their god. They were the face of the god being represented to the people on earth.

The same idea is being conveyed in verse 26. We are made as the images of God for our planet, and the verse continues, "And let them have dominion over the fish of the sea and over the birds of the heavens and over the livestock and over all the earth and over every creeping thing that creeps on the earth."

God has called us to be his representative, to continue the creation he started.

———————————————

The Bible tells the story of God's work in the world, and man's place in it. Genesis one and two tell of what God did before us. In that time, God created. He then chose us to be his representatives, to continue that creation.

The beginning was a garden. The end, according to Revelation, is a city. That's the flow of humanity. That's what God has called us to do. To take the world he created, and make things out of it. Subdue the earth — take its materials, and make things ourselves.

In addition to that, we are meant to procreate, to make more people, like he's made us. All of this is miraculous, it's a God-like work. The miracle of birth, and the miracle of work.

Work is not bad. Work is *not* part of the curse. Work is more difficult because of the curse, but it is part of God's perfect creation.

In the afterlife, we won't be free from work. It's always been a part of God's plan, and always will be. It's part of his nature, and we are to be like him. Work will become pure joy, heavenly.

I am, notoriously, opposed to manual labor.

My dad has done construction for nearly all my life. He owns his own business, building houses and other buildings.

Every summer I would be forced to work with him. He'd wake me up every morning (while it was still dark, I should note) and drag my older brother and me with him to whatever job we had that day.

I like sleep. I always have. So it was quite a chore to get up every morning and go to work. I'd sleep in the truck on the way to the job site. Sleep on the way to lunch and back. And then I'd sleep on the way home.

To be honest, I hated nearly every minute of that work. I don't like the outdoors. It's hot. I despise sawdust. I don't have a high tolerance for pain. And I'm not particularly strong. Also, I just wasn't very good at it.

Talk to me about an idea. Let me research a topic and teach it to you. Those are my skills.

Manual labor — not happening. I'll use the money I make from all these book sales and call someone to fix it.

My dad on the other hand, he can fix anything. Now that I don't live at home anymore, going back is enlightening. I can see my dad from a new point of view.

He's one of those people who is always doing something. The rest of us will hang out in the living room of my parents' house and talk, or watch a movie, and he'll be off fixing a car, or working in a garden, or mowing a lawn, or, now that he's a pastor, working on a sermon.

He doesn't even stop at his own stuff. He'll mow his mother's lawn, his in-laws', the Little League's, the church's. He doesn't stop.

My dad and I, while very much alike in our demeanor, couldn't be more different in the things we create.

He'd rather build a house than write a book. And I'd rather die than build a house. (Not really, but I'd definitely rather write a book.)

The joy of the modern day is that creation can happen in a ridiculous number of ways.

There are people who simply create digital products, things that never make it to the physical world. Fifty years ago that would have been unimaginable.

Our modern world has also given us the ability to create nonessential things as a career. There are people who write books or make movies and music for a living.

But with that has come a twisted view of art. Since there are people who create art for a living, we have restricted art to its own arena and made everything else pure utility.

When archaeologists excavate the remains of ancient civilizations, they often find tools that had engravings, or paintings, or something on them that made them beautiful.

Humanity is meant to create, and since the beginning of time, humans have. We've made beautiful things. Since ancient people couldn't make careers out of painting, they would paint their tools. Since they couldn't make a career out of music, their times of gathering were filled with song.

Since they couldn't make art their life, they made their life art.

That's a subtle distinction, but it's important. While utility is good, beauty shouldn't be lost.

———

Have you ever stopped to wonder why we see color in the world?

Why would God make color such a staple of his creation? It didn't have to be that way. It doesn't serve a significant utilitarian purpose.

He did it because it is beautiful. This means that, to God, beauty is an inherently good thing. Beauty, in and of itself, is a good for which we should strive.

What does this mean for your work? Well, it means you should strive for beauty. Whatever you do, do it to the best of your ability. Do it in a way that glorifies God. Recognize that what you do, while it may not seem like it, is probably art. It's something that requires skill, imagination, and nuance. It's something you can do better. It's something you can think more deeply about.

Like God, we are all creators. It's our job, as his image bearers in the world, to subdue the earth — to create, to redeem, to make beautiful.

Chapter 8

How do you view your time?

"You have to deeply understand the essence of the product in order to be able to get rid of the parts that are not essential."

Jony Ive

Have you ever seen the movie *In Time*? It came out in 2011 and starred Justin Timberlake and Amanda Seyfried. The story is set in a dystopian world where time is the currency. Each person lives until they are 25, and then they stop aging. The problem is that at 25 they are only allotted one more year of time. They can earn more, but they also have to spend it to live. Everything they purchase takes away a little bit of their life. A coffee costs a few minutes. The rich gamble years.

The poor run everywhere, because they don't have time to waste. The rich walk leisurely, because they've got plenty to last them centuries.

Even though it's fictional, this movie gives a great picture of how we should view our time.

We budget our money, we pay attention to how we spend it. And in the Christian world, there are books upon books about finances and how to manage money as a Christian. The question is, Why don't we treat our time the same way?

Time is a currency we are constantly spending. We devote every moment we have to spending time. This, I think, makes it our most valuable currency. It makes our time the currency we should be most focused on. You can always make more money, but you can't make more time.

Imagine you had a bank account that had a set amount of money. Once you ran out you would be done. You couldn't make any more.

You would probably plan how you spent it a little better. You'd budget it. You would make long term and short term goals for your money. You'd take it incredibly seriously.

As Christians, we should do the same with our time — paying more attention to how we spend it.

To be honest, I am incredibly bad at this. I am one of the laziest people I know. I always have been. I really have to work at being productive, at making the most of my time, at not procrastinating. But I know the times in my life I was most productive are the times in my life where I felt most satisfied. I felt closest to God. I felt like I had meaning. And I know I'm not the only one.

If I feel that way when I'm being productive, and if I have the desire and the feeling of moral obligation to make the most of my time, it may mean that that is how God created me to live. And the same goes for you. I'm sure you have the pull inside of you, this urge, telling you that you should do something with your life. This feeling that you don't have forever, that you need to accomplish something meaningful.

I believe God placed that in us, because He wants us to do great things. He wants us to make things, to meet people, to change lives. He wants us to change the world. He doesn't want us to waste our time here on earth.

In the movie, Justin Timberlake's character is very poor. He rarely has more than a day left to spend. He's constantly trying to make more and save more, so he doesn't run out. But he's given over a century by a very wealthy man who has had enough of life. He had already lived a century when they met.

The man gives him the time while Timberlake's character is sleeping. And when he wakes up, he sees written on the window near him:

"Don't waste my time."

I believe God has done the same with us. He has given us time on this earth to accomplish something of value, to glorify Him. And I think He's telling us, "Don't waste my time."

To be honest, writing that makes me feel a little odd. Putting it in those kinds of words makes God sound cold and heartless. Like he's a cruel coach up in the sky, getting angry when we're on the couch watching Seinfeld.

I don't think he's like that, and that's not what I mean when I say he doesn't want us to waste time.

The Christian vision is gracious. God knows what humans are like. He knows we fail. And that's why we have Christ. He's telling us to not waste his time, not in the way a heartless coach would, but a loving father. He wants us to not waste his time because he wants the best for us, not because he's worried about his time. And part of not wasting it is enjoying it. So sometimes watching Seinfeld is a good thing. (At least I hope so. I've spent a lot of time watching Seinfeld...)

As Christians, we need to internalize the importance of doing something that matters, of spending our time wisely. But we also need to know that that's not what Christianity is about. It's important for us to accomplish much, but also to realize accomplishment does not equal fulfillment. We need that balance.

God cares most about loving you, not using you. The Gospel is not about accomplishing more than those around us. It's about a relationship with God. But, the Gospel does push us to do more, *because* of our relationship with God.

As Christians, we need to be smart with our time. We need to know it has value. Even though we'll have eternity after our time here, that doesn't mean we can waste it.

Jony Ive, Chief Design Officer at Apple once said this: "You have to deeply understand the essence of the product in order to be able to get rid of the parts that are not essential."[10] Ive is responsible for the designs of nearly every successful product at Apple. He's a genius. And this philosophy, while about creating products, is incredibly applicable to the creation of our lives.

The problem with time is knowing how to spend it. You can understand the importance of spending it wisely, but the question remains, "What is wise?" This depends completely on the person. It's not something anybody can figure out for you. That's what makes it so difficult.

What I can tell you is that, just like Ive's products, you have to understand the essence of it before you can cut out the parts that are not essential.

You must first figure out what the essence of your life is. What is it you are trying to accomplish? What is it

God has created you to do? Once you've figured that out, you can shape your time around it.

Chapter 9

How do you treat those with whom you disagree?

"Apologetics should be done with humble boldness. Don't give an inch on truth, but buy the next cup of coffee..."

Cornelius Van Til

Arguing has always been a major part of my life. Just ask my parents...

But seriously. I love to argue, and most of the time, when I got in trouble with my parents, it was for "talking back." Yes, I probably went about it the wrong way when I was younger, but the point is, it's in my nature to argue.

Well, it's in my nature to critique, to find fault, to know the error in reasoning. It's just that now I am

90

slightly better at knowing when to offer my contradiction, and when to hold back.

Slightly.

I still have a hard time. I often contradict my wife just for the sake of contradicting. She'll tell me a dog is white, and for some reason, I have to tell her, "Well, it's mostly white. It does have that patch of grey hair... there... on its left hind foot... about a centimeter in diameter..."

But this critical nature, like most things that are our weaknesses in personality, is also my strength. Yes, I have a hard time finding the good in something, and letting go of the bad. But I am very good at discerning what is true, and what is not. This flaw that is also a feature is what has made me who I am. And it has made me pretty good at arguing. Which is what we are going to talk about next.

Christians often cringe at the thought of someone having an argument. Most say, or at least think, arguing is bad.

I disagree.*

The image often conjured up in the minds of Christians when the thought of an argument appears is one of two people angry at each other. Maybe yelling, or at least speaking very firmly. Whatever is happening, they know it is unproductive. Both sides of the argument are sticking to their views and aren't budging one bit. People are getting hurt.

If this is the definition of an argument, then I totally agree, we shouldn't do it. But that's not what arguing is — at least it doesn't have to be.

Here are a few different online dictionary definitions of the word "argue":

---

* Probably the least revelatory statement in this book.

Dictionary.com: to present reasons for or against a thing

thefreedictionary.com: to put forth reasons for or against; debate

Merriam-webster.com: to give reasons for or against something

Arguing is just giving reasons for or against something. The word does not necessarily mean that it must be done angrily or unkindly.

Think of it this way. Your view of the world is like a map. It tells you where everything is and how to get there. And just like a physical map, your mental map, if wrong, will lead you astray. To be corrected, you must have someone come in and show you their map. They have to show how it lines up more with reality. Once that happens, you can update your map and get back on the right course. The frequent comparing of maps can help you, and those around you, stay on course.

Each person has a view of the world around them. They have a view of what you should and shouldn't do, what is and isn't true about reality. Arguing is comparing those mental maps, trying to determine which one fits with reality more.

And oftentimes, because we are human, we are going to be wrong. But we shouldn't throw in the towel.

The Bible tells us about the importance of truth. Our own desires tell us about the importance of truth. We all long for it. If truth is so important we should be dedicated to discovering. But searching it out means relying on others to help us.

To help us by comparing maps, by arguing.

It doesn't have to be a hard process. If you have the right motives, the discovery of truth by the correction of a friend can be a good experience. When comparing maps, your goal should be to know the truth about the world, even if the other person has it.

Arguing isn't about being right; it's about coming to know what's right and helping others do the same.

Our maps shouldn't be written in ink.

Wherever the truth is, it is necessary to find it. And you have to compare mental maps to do it. You have to argue.

———————

As a general rule, humans are terrible at this. Which is part of the reason why we tend to retreat back into our little groups, constantly complaining about the other side, rather than getting to know what they actually think.

We tend to hold caricatures of the other side's view, rather than the actual thing. Then we toss our beliefs back and forth, never actually getting anywhere.

These caricatures are incredibly harmful. They're lies we tell ourselves. And for some reason, they're lies we're not too worried about correcting.

Harmful may be a soft word for that.

Think of it this way…

Ideas look like branches. All ideas stem from other ideas. If you are trying to figure out what someone thinks, move a little further down the tree. You'll learn a lot.

For example, let's say my wife makes the claim that a particular salad is fantastic, I respond with the claim that it is, in fact, not. At this moment, we realize we disagree. We then begin to argue.

Here are her reasons:

1. The lettuce is crisp and fresh.

2. The croutons are crunchy and have a lot of flavor.

3. The dressing is rich and creamy, better than any she has had before.

4. This, therefore, means the salad is tasty.

I am not convinced.

The problem is she could argue those points all day and I would still not be convinced. Not because those aren't good reasons, but because the reasons don't line up with a more basic belief that I hold.

Her appeal to the freshness of the lettuce is great. That's a valid criterion for lettuce. The problem is that I don't like lettuce at all. I don't like the flavor of any lettuce, no matter how crisp and fresh it is. So the argument will never convince me.

Her argument for the goodness of the salad can only work if I first get to the point where I accept the goodness of lettuce. Until then, arguing about the freshness of the lettuce is completely useless.

Let's look at a more political example — abortion.

The topic of abortion is an important one. And the debate is charged and practically endless.

(Do note that this example is a little different than the salad. Abortion not an issue of preference, but of morality — of truth.)

One of the major problems with the debate on abortion is that we don't really understand why people think what they think. When the topic comes up, it's typically a fruitless back and forth about women's rights. The question most often asked and argued is, "Does a woman have the right to end a pregnancy?"

Now, this is a good question, but it doesn't get to the heart of the question for most pro-life people. For pro-lifers, the more basic, and important question is, "Is the unborn a human being?"

The pro-life person is not against women's rights. They just think that nobody has the right to kill a human being without proper justification. And the unborn is a human being.

98

And on the other side, the pro-choice advocate is not in support of killing babies, they just don't (normally) believe the unborn are real human beings. So for them, the question then becomes, "Does a woman have the right to end the growth of something inside their body?"

So if you are pro-choice, you'll never convince your pro-life friend of your view by talking about a woman's right to control her body. For the pro-lifer, the life of a human being is almost always more important.

Disagreement on any topic often stems from a disagreement much lower in the branches of belief. When you disagree, find the source.

This is also why we are often baffled by a person's beliefs. If your assumption is that the unborn are human, then someone supporting abortion seems illogical at best, and immensely immoral at worst. But if you understand that there is something further down the belief branch that is probably causing the disagreement, you'll realize they're not crazy or immoral, they just believe differently.

You see, the pro-choice advocate is not a baby killer.

The pro-lifer is not against women's rights.

The theistic evolutionist is not anti-Bible.

The creationist is not anti-science.

The Arminian is not ignoring the text.

The Calvinist isn't uncaring.

If you "have no idea why" a person would think what they think, you probably aren't listening.

You probably aren't asking enough questions. You're probably more interested in proving them wrong than understanding their position. Rather than moving down the branches, you're probably assuming you are starting at the same branch and they are making a leap somewhere else, into irrationality.

If they seem crazy for not liking the salad, make sure they actually like lettuce. Your arguments will be a lot more fruitful. (Or *vegetable*, am I right?)* Only when you get to the root of the problem will you be able to have a meaningful conversation.

As Christians, we're called to love our neighbors. Loving your neighbor means doing your best to get to know them.

To get past the caricature. To eradicate the lie.

We're never going to have an impact on our culture if we keep pushing our ideas without honestly listening to our neighbor's.

---

* So sorry.

Listen. Have a conversation. Love your neighbor. Be bold, but be humble. "Don't give an inch on truth, but buy the next cup of coffee."[11]

Part 3:

Going Forward

Chapter 10

Actions and Words

"Now at Iconium they entered together into the Jewish synagogue and spoke in such a way that a great number of both Jews and Greeks believed."

Acts 14:1

There is a quotation that floats its way around every so often, it's this:

"Preach the Gospel at all times, and if necessary use words."

The quotation is often attributed to St. Francis of Assisi. And it's a nice sounding quote. It's nice and Christian-y.

Another one often used in conjunction with it is the now clichéd "Actions speak louder than words."

I technically agree with both of those. The problem is, they're most often used to make a point I *don't* agree with. The point is that the most important way for us to share the Gospel is through our actions. That words aren't often necessary.

This, I think, is very, very wrong. And here's why:

There are a lot of people out there who like to play charades. (They're a little odd, but, you know, to each his own.)

The reason charades is so (supposedly) fun to play is that *it's difficult to interpret someone's actions*. The point of the game is to try to communicate an idea without using words, because it's easier to communicate with words than without.

Yes, actions speak louder than words... But we can't stop there.

Actions may speak louder, but words speak clearer. To effectively communicate you have to have both.

We need both pillars of intelligent faith. We need the clear message of intelligent belief, but we also need the resounding megaphone of intelligent living.

Without the megaphone, we won't be heard. We may know what we're talking about, but we'll never reach anyone. But without the message, our action will be meaningless — just another noise in an already blaring world.

In the next chapter, I'll tell you the story of a man named William Wilberforce. Wilberforce did not separate his words from his actions. Part of his appeal was that he was an immensely elegant speaker. He was witty and powerful. Not only did he commit the actions in his life to the cause he was called to accomplish, but he powerfully used words to argue the necessity of the changes he was attempting to make. His debates in the British parliament were just as necessary as his moral life in attaining the end he was called to.

The example of Jesus displays this as well. He lived a powerful life. A life of love toward the outcast, the marginalized. He loved everyone he came in contact with. He did miracles. He stood up for the oppressed.

He also spoke eloquently. He used words to convey the message he wanted people to hear. He preached *along with* raising the dead. He told parables *as* he healed the sick. He did not compartmentalize his approach and neither should we.

The intelligent Christian will live, and speak, in a way that causes those who don't believe to question their unbelief. The intelligent Christian will live, and speak, in a way that glorifies the God we serve.

Chapter 11

The Example of William Wilberforce

"Christianity is not a series of truths in the plural, but rather truth spelled with a capital 'T.' Truth about all of reality, not just religious things."

Francis Shaeffer

When starting the brand of *Don't be stupid.*, we talked to a designer about creating a logo. The designer and I went back and forth quite a bit about what this logo should look like. I told her what the concept was about, and she attempted to create something that portrayed it in the form of an image.

Since the whole idea is being a smart Christian, we went through several iterations of a brain, cast in different forms. What we ended up with is the lightbulb you see on the cover of this book.

This lightbulb, as you've probably noticed, has a heart in the middle of it. The lightbulb is a symbol of ideas, of thoughts, of intelligence. The heart is the symbol of love.

These two cannot be separated. Much like we can't compartmentalize our actions and words, we must also hold together our intelligence with our love.

The idea of *Don't be stupid.* is not simply to be smart. It's intelligence, fueled by love.

The Bible says that as Christians, we should be known by our love. We can also see this in the example of Christ. People were drawn to him because he cared for them, genuinely and wholeheartedly.

Another man in history who modeled this well is a man named William Wilberforce.

William Wilberforce was born in England, in the port city of Hull. He was born in 1759. His family was a prosperous family. They, and the people around them had high hopes for Wilberforce, and he exceeded those expectations.

Within months of graduating from Cambridge University he secured a seat in the House of Commons as a member of Parliament for Hull — just a few days after his 21st birthday.

During this time, he became great friends with William Pitt the Younger. Pitt eventually became the youngest Prime Minister in British history.

They were both gifted beyond measure. Wilberforce was witty, had a brilliant intellect, and was known as a masterful orator with the most beautiful of voices.

They both quickly ascended in the ranks of Parliament over the next few years. After an important election to a very high level of Parliament, Wilberforce decided to go on a trip around the country. He invited with him a man named Isaac Milner. Most likely, the reason Wilberforce invited him was that Milner was arguably the most brilliant man in England at the time.

He was a Fellow of the Royal Society. A title also held by men like Isaac Newton, and now Stephen Hawking. Milner was a massive man, in intellect, and frame.

He also happened to be a Christian.

Along with, I'm sure, many other incredibly interesting discussions, one of the topics they covered while traveling was the topic of Christianity.* Wilberforce was not a Christian at this time. He actually mocked it.

But over the course of this trip he was becoming more and more worried that this worldview was not as absurd as he once thought.

---

* If I could travel back in time, looking in on these conversations is most definitely one of the things I would do. Although, that might not be too smart. Nobody really knows what happens to time when you start messing with things. We could have some Flashpoint craziness happening here... Never mind.

When he arrived back home he began to contemplate what he believed. He wondered, could this religion he mocked actually be true? He agonized over the question for what probably felt like an eternity.

This question posed a problem for many reasons. First, Wilberforce wanted to believe what was true. He wanted to know what reality was, and for his beliefs to fit it. He didn't want to believe a lie, so it was important to him to figure out, not just did he want to believe it, but was it true.

Second, in this era, people believed that to be truly committed to God meant to remove yourself from society. It was thought that to be a true Christian, you must go into ministry, or become a monk — politics was not an option for a Christian.

This meant that Wilberforce was not just making a decision about beliefs, but his future. He was already incredibly influential in his government, and had hopes to do so much more. He was good at it, and he didn't want to give it up. But, he never did anything half-way, so if he were to become a Christian, he was going to go all in.

Eventually, after many hours of contemplation, and a number of conversations with his childhood pastor, John Newton*, he finally came to the conclusion that Christianity was true, and he was going to dedicate his life to it.

So while already well on his way to becoming one of the most powerful men in England, he was leaving politics.

He wrote a letter to his best friend, William Pitt, explaining his decision. This, I'm sure, must have been agonizing.

I imagine him sitting at his desk, quill in hand, ink beside the paper, writing this letter. His stomach is

---

* John Newton was a former slave ship captain, and the eventual writer of the hymn, *Amazing Grace*.

sinking, heart pounding, sweat in his palms, tears in his eyes. He's breaking the news to his best friend, his ally in life, and in politics — telling him he's no longer going to be there with him. Their days of debating together, lobbying together, rising the ranks of the nation together, are over. He's becoming a Christian.

Pitt's response was impressive, especially for not being a Christian himself.

Pitt was already planning his rise to Prime Minister, and needed Wilberforce's help to do that. His letter was understanding. He told him he would respect whatever decision Wilberforce made. He really knew Wilberforce, and it showed in this letter.

But he also offered Wilberforce a challenge.

Pitt pushed Wilberforce to reconsider his decision to leave politics. He gave several reasons:

Number one, he told him that this would "render your virtues and your talents useless both to yourself and mankind."[12] He believed that Wilberforce had great potential, and to leave politics would be to do a disservice to mankind, to waste his God-given talents.

He then appealed to Wilberforce's view of religion. Wilberforce must have mentioned some of his beliefs about religion in his letter to Pitt, because Pitt uses them to argue his point.

He points out that Wilberforce believes religion does not lead to a gloomy outlook on life, but also not an overly optimistic one. Pitt argues that a life of solitude can only lead to one of these two extremes. He asks him, "But why then this preparation of solitude, which can hardly avoid tincturing the mind either with melancholy or superstition?"[13]

In my opinion, a well formulated argument. Like I said, he knows Wilberforce, and he knows how to persuade.

He ends this series of challenges with a magnificent finish. He writes, "Surely the principles as well as the practice of Christianity are simple, and lead not to meditation only but to action."[14]

―――――――――

After this letter and much thought, Wilberforce decided his Christian life was best served in the correction of the evils of his world.

Life in eighteenth-century Britain was particularly brutal, decadent, violent, and vulgar. Slavery was only the worst of a host of societal evils that included epidemic alcoholism, child prostitution, child labor, frequent public executions for petty crimes, public dissections and burnings of executed criminals, and unfathomable cruelty to animals.

In 1787, Wilberforce wrote in his journal, "God Almighty has set before me two great objects, the suppression of the Slave Trade and the Reformation of Manners."[15]

And so, even as Wilberforce waged what would be a 20-year fight to abolish Britain's slave trade, he began scores of philanthropic initiatives. Some estimate *almost 70 separate causes* were significantly advanced by the influence of Wilberforce.[16]

After his fight against the slave trade ended in 1807, he began working against slavery as a whole. This one, too, was a long and difficult battle, due to the massive economy behind it and his near constant illness. Finally, in 1833, a bill outlawing slavery in Britain and all its colonies was passed.

Wilberforce died the next day.

Reading his story makes one think Wilberforce was superhuman. (And to be honest, I'm not entirely convinced he wasn't.)

Thomas Jefferson and Abraham Lincoln both praised Wilberforce as an inspiration and example. Lincoln said every schoolboy knew Wilberforce's name and what he had done. Frederick Douglass said that Wilberforce's "faith, persistence, and enduring enthusiasm" had "thawed the British heart into sympathy for the slave, and moved the strong arm of that government to, in mercy, put an end to his bondage."

But even mere mortals can learn from the accomplishments of those greater than us. Wilberforce is no different.

The first lesson we can learn is that Christianity is not an escape from, but an engagement to culture. The clichéd phrase "Be in the world, but not of it" is actually sound advice.

Many believe, as Wilberforce did, that to become a Christian meant to depart from the culture. The culture, mind you, is depraved, and contagious in its depravity. But the Gospel is powerful. It's more powerful than we could ever imagine.

Because of this, our fear of entering the culture is unfounded. As many have pointed out, Jesus himself did not seclude himself from culture. He engaged it in an intentional and meaningful way.

Wilberforce, after his change of mind, did the same. He realized that to engage culture was more Christian than to escape it.

———

Have you ever wondered why this tendency we have to escape culture is so strong?

Well, it all goes back to Plato.

Plato had this theory about the world. His theory split things into Matter and Form. Matter is the things we see, the tables, the chairs, the trees. But these things are just representations, shadows, of the Form of that thing in the immaterial (or spiritual) world.

So, in the immaterial world, there is a Form of tableness, *that* is true tableness. Our tables are just a shadow of true tableness. They are good, but they are not the ultimate good.

What does this mean in practice? Well, it means that the spiritual is good, the physical is not as good. Even further than that, things like art are bad. If a tree is a copy of something, a painting of the tree, for instance, is a copy of a copy — so far removed from the good, it can't be beneficial.

This mindset, while not present in the same way as Plato, has infiltrated many cultures throughout history. Paul, in his New Testament writings was often responding to Gnostics, a people who believed the physical world was bad, and the way to God was through a spiritual knowledge.

In our culture it has risen again, in subtler, but still significant ways. How often do we elevate positions in "ministry," and shun the more "worldly" work? So many teens, as soon as they become Christians, feel a pressure to devote their lives to ministry.

We also disregard art as valuable, or beauty as meaningful. While, as we learned in an earlier chapter, God obviously values beauty.

Francis Shaeffer wrote about this problem. He called it the sacred/secular split. What he pushed for is a view of Christianity as "total truth." Shaeffer once wrote, "Christianity is not a series of truths in the plural, but rather truth spelled with a capital 'T.' Truth about all of reality, not just religious things."[18]

Our Christianity applies to every aspect of our lives, from what church we go to, all the way to how we buy a car. Along with that, it calls us to engage culture. To get our hands dirty.

Wilberforce definitely left this world with some dirt on his hands.

That leads us to the next thing we can learn from Wilberforce — he didn't shy away from the tough issues. He simply did what he believed God wanted him to, even though it threatened the bedrock of the British economy.

The issue was provocative, it was crazy, it was wildly out of reach. But he did it. He didn't shy away.

Not only that, but he worked and worked and worked, until the job was done. He was focused on doing good, no matter the consequence, no matter the cost.

The American artist and inventor Samuel Morse, who lived at the time of Wilberforce said that Wilberforce's "whole soul is bent on doing good to his fellow men. Not a moment of his time is lost. He is always planning some benevolent scheme, or other, and not only planning but executing…. Oh, that such men as Mr. Wilberforce were more common in this world."

"He was always planning some benevolent scheme." Man, would I like that to be my epitaph.

The third thing we can learn from Wilberforce is the importance of community.

God works in community. He started with a nation, Israel. Jesus had his disciples. He then created the Church. Community has always been how God worked in this world, but it's also part of his nature.

As Christians we believe in a triune God — a God who exists in three persons. This means that from eternity God has existed in community. It's his nature, and he planted that in us.

Wilberforce modeled this. He was part of a group called the Clapham Sect. They lived together in a small community, they worked together to fight the battles in their culture. Without them, Wilberforce never would have accomplished what he did.

We often assume our callings are personal callings, but they never are. They are callings to take part in something bigger, to be a part of a community that does good work, not to do the work alone.

Like Wilberforce (and like our creator), we must live in community.

———————————

Finally, I do want to mention that Wilberforce was fun. He was a cool guy, and people loved him. A contemporary of Wilberforce, Gerard Edwards, wrote, "I thank God that I live in the age of Wilberforce and that I know one man at least who is both moral and entertaining."

I hope to live in a culture where people long to be around Christians, like people longed to be around Wilberforce. (And around Jesus, for that matter.)

May we be like Wilberforce — engaging our culture, with unwavering fervor, alongside a tight-knit community, who are attractive to the people around them.

Chapter 12

The Example of C. S. Lewis

"Men despise religion. They hate it and are afraid it may be true. The cure for this is first to show that religion is not contrary to reason, but worthy of reverence and respect.

Next make it attractive, make good men wish it were true, then show that it is.

Worthy of reverence because it really understands human nature.

Attractive because it promises true good."

Blaise Pascal

You know when you're reading a book and you come across a long quotation? Are you one of those people who just skips over it, assuming you'll get the gist?

Well, you're probably right. Chances are, the author will summarize. He'll take the quotation he just tossed in the middle of his chapter, and he'll tell you what it means. So, you think, "What's the point of reading it myself?"

I want to encourage you to *not* do that during this chapter. We're about to talk about a man who was a magnificent writer. One who the author of this book greatly admires, yet doesn't compare to one bit. So when we get to those points where I do the thing where I drop a paragraph from another author, please don't skip it. Even though I will probably summarize it after, to make sure you get the point, the point will be made *so* much better by the guy I'm quoting…

And that guy, his name is C. S. Lewis.

C. S. Lewis believed that within five years after his death he would be forgotten. Fifty years later we know he was most obviously wrong. His book *Mere*

Christianity is on nearly every "recommended reading" list of every apologetic website you find. His scholarly work in the field of Medieval and Renaissance literary criticism is still used in universities today. And his fiction is still selling like mad — *The Chronicles of Narnia* have sold over 100 million copies in 47 languages.

So, what makes C. S. Lewis so great?

It's not that he was perfect. He was far from it. Some of his views are a bit edgy. And some of the things he did wouldn't fly in today's church culture.*

I think what made C. S. Lewis great was that he didn't just tell people the facts about Christianity, he gave them images that displayed the beauty of what Christianity is. He made people want Christianity to be true (Like in *The Chronicles of Narnia*) and then showed them that it was (Like in *Mere Christianity*).

---

* His odd marriage arrangement didn't fly well in his culture either.

And he did all of this artistically — with poetry, fiction, and imagery.

He wasn't dry. He wasn't boring. His writing is intellectually rigorous, yet poetically beautiful. It's smart, but witty.

———————————

We live in a culture that doesn't want to hear about Christianity. And we live in a culture that has a lot of intellectual questions.

But they're sound bite questions. The questions aren't typically ones they got from reading a book on philosophy. They read it in a blog, or saw it on YouTube.

In a culture like that, we need artful pictures of Christianity, not purely prosaic ones. Our culture won't sit around for a sermon on why Christianity is true, but they may listen to an entertaining podcast.

They probably won't read your 250 page book, but they may watch your well-made YouTube video.

What made Lewis great, I think, is that he was a model for how Christians should engage culture. He was a model for an intelligent Christian.

In his essay entitled "Christian Apologetics," Lewis wrote this:

> We must attack the enemy's line of communication. What we want is not more little books about Christianity, but more little books by Christians on other subjects — with their Christianity latent. You can see this most easily if you look at it the other way round. Our faith is not likely to be shaken by any book on Hinduism. But if whenever we read an elementary book on geology, botany, politics, or astronomy, we found that its implications were Hindu, that would shake us. It is not the books written in direct defense of materialism that make the modern man a materialist: it is the materialistic assumptions in all the other books. In the same way, it is not books on Christianity that will really trouble him. But he would be troubled if whenever

> he wanted a cheap popular introduction to some
> science, the best work on the market was always by
> a Christian. The first step to the reconversion of a
> country is books produced by Christians.[21]

(You didn't skip, did you? Jesus is watching.)

In addition to "when he wanted a cheap popular introduction to some science," you could add, "when he wanted some good music, the best was always made by a Christian," or "when he needed a doctor, the best was always a Christian," or "when he wanted to buy life insurance," or "when he wanted to read a good novel."

The list could go on and on. The point is, I'm being somewhat hypocritical in writing this — because what Lewis and I are saying is that books like this one are not really the solution. The explicitly Christian books and music and movies and businesses have their place. But they will not change our culture. The change will come when the most respected content in our culture is made with the assumptions of the Christian worldview as the bedrock.

I say C. S. Lewis is a model because he did this exact thing. He wrote explicitly Christian works like *Mere Christianity*, there is a place for them, but he also wrote works like *The Chronicles of Narnia*. When someone reads *The Chronicles of Narnia*, they don't think, "Okay, I'm about to read this Christian book." No, most people don't know it was written by a Christian. They just know they are good books.

But when people read them, they are drawn into a world that has the Christian worldview as its foundation. They encounter concepts like sacrifice, redemption, forgiveness, repentance, beauty, goodness, and truth. They are drawn into this world because it's interesting, because it is fun, because it is beautiful.

Our culture has heard the story of Jesus so many times they have become immune to it. Telling them the same message over and over is going to do them no good. But when they can encounter it in a new way, they have the opportunity to see the truth of it, not the cultural baggage-laden conception of it they currently hold.

What these books do, and other works like them, is help people encounter Christianity in a fresh way, pushing past their assumptions about it.

Lewis, in an essay about writing "fairy stories," put it this way:

> I thought I saw how stories of this kind could steal past a certain inhibition which had paralysed much of my own religion in childhood. Why did one find it so hard to feel as one was told one ought to feel about God or about the sufferings of Christ? I thought the chief reason was that one was told one ought to. An obligation to feel can freeze feelings. And reverence itself did harm. The whole subject was associated with lowered voices; almost as if it were something medical. But supposing that by casting all these things into an imaginary world, stripping them of their stained-glass and Sunday school associations, one could make them for the first time appear in their real potency? Could one not thus steal past those watchful dragons? I thought one could.[22]

What Lewis is saying is that, in writing fiction, you get the chance to sneak by the assumptions held by your audience. You could shoot past the feelings they have about "religion." And by doing that, you could present them in a way that gave them back their real power.

Toward the end of *The Voyage of the Dawn Treader*, the third book in the series,· this dialogue occurs, at a point where Lucy and Edmund are distraught at the revelation that they will not be returning to Narnia.

> "It isn't Narnia, you know," sobbed Lucy. "It's you. We shan't meet you there. And how can we live, never meeting you?"
>
> "But you shall meet me, dear one," said Aslan.
>
> "Are — are you there too, Sir?" said Edmund.
>
> "I am," said Aslan. "But there I have another name. You must learn to know me by that name. This was the very reason why you were brought to Narnia,

---

* Or the fifth, if you hold to the incorrect ordering of the books.

that by knowing me here for a little, you may know me better there."[23]

Lewis is hinting to the reader that there is an Aslan-like figure here as well. He's showing them, rather than telling them about the beauty of Christ.

He's giving the reader an amazing story. A story that draws them in. A story that makes them long for Narnia, and for Aslan in particular. Then showing them, rather than explicitly telling them, they can actually have Aslan.

They don't have to long for Narnia, they are in it. They don't have to long for Aslan, they can have him. He is in their world as well.

By being brought to Narnia you're given a glimpse of something you might not have wished to encounter otherwise. The "watchful dragons" would have prevented the occurrence. But Lewis, by creating something of great quality, not explicitly Christian, but latent with the Christian worldview, stole past them.

Jesus did this same kind of thing. His parables are beautiful, poetic stories that are much more powerful and memorable than the mere statement of facts.

We must do this as well. Only then will people start wanting to listen. If we keep doing the same stupid thing over and over again, we'll keep on getting the same crappy results.

For example, nobody wants to be told to "accept Jesus into their hearts," ever again. That phrase is worn. It has no meaning.

My challenge to you is to do amazing things. Create innovative companies, design awesome websites, build beautiful houses. Do your job in a way that reflects the beauty of the Christian message. Only when our culture begins to see the beauty and power of the Christian message will they begin to take it seriously.

That's being an intelligent Christian — displaying the beauty, and then presenting the truth, of the Gospel of Christ.

Chapter 13

A Guide to Intelligent Christianity

"No one expects to attain to the height of learning, or arts, or power, or wealth, or military glory, without vigorous resolution, strenuous diligence, and steady perseverance. Yet we expect to be Christians without labour, study, or inquiry."

William Wilberforce

The question now, as we're drawing near the end, is how do we do this? Is it really possible for every Christian to not be stupid?

As someone who is really into this apologetics and theology stuff, I know it may come across to someone else that this is easy for me. I know that if I were on the other end, the one reading this book, this is what I'd be thinking:

137

You know what? You keep telling me that I need to do all of this stuff. That I need to learn all of this, and I need to make great things, but I honestly don't have that kind of time. For you it's easy. This is your job. My job is to be an engineer, a contractor, or an accountant. I don't have time to read hundreds of books. I don't have time to do something that I'll be remembered for. It's just not practical.

Now, on the surface, if you're thinking that, I would agree with you. I would say you're right, you are not me. You are not someone that's making a career out of learning and teaching theology and philosophy. I *should* be spending my time doing this stuff. And the accountant's time should be spent learning about and doing accounting.

But this is not what I'm saying. I don't think God requires every Christian to be an expert in apologetics. And I don't think God calls every Christian to do something that "changes the world" in the sense that thousands of people will know about you. But, I do think that God requires every single Christian to know the basics of apologetics. Every single Christian should be able to answer the question, "Why are you a Christian?"

The Bible clearly states that you should be ready to give a reason for the hope that you have. It doesn't say that you need to be able to answer every question someone tosses your way. But you should be able to start, to have some good reasons, and then be able to help find the answers when the questions come up.

And as far as everyday life goes, I'm not saying that every Christian should have such an impact that they reach thousands of people. What I'm saying is that whatever they do, they should do it to the best of their ability. They should make the most of their time. They should be smart about how they go about their day. That's all I'm asking. And that's all the Bible requires. But even though I say "that's all" I don't mean it's a small feat. It still takes work. But it's good work. It's fulfilling work. And it's work that brings joy to you and your Creator.

So, you can do it. And here is how.

1. Take the time to learn.

At the heart of an intelligent faith is a curious faith. If you commit to asking questions, you will become more intelligent. Curiosity may have killed the cat, but I'd rather die learning than live in stupidity.

What kinds of things should you ask questions about? What do you need to learn about?

Here are some things to start with.

Learn about your faith.

Figure out why you believe what you believe. Ask questions about the Bible. Ask questions about the nature of God.

I've found that the more I know about God, the more I'm astounded at who he is. The more I know about him, the more I sit in wonder at his grace, his power, and the more thankful I am for him.

That's definitely a good place for a Christian to be.

Learn about your work.

Whatever it is you do for a living, do it to the best of your ability. In order to do that, you need to learn about it. If you are salesperson, read books about sales. Learn how to master your craft. Make it an act of worship. Whatever you do, learn how to do it right.

When we have a country of Christians who are doing what they do incredibly well, people will take notice. And it will bring glory to God — the ultimate creator. The one who does everything with love, care, and perfection.

In your work, mimic the Great Worker.

Learn about your hobbies.
Any kind of learning is beneficial. And it's good for us to have hobbies. It's good for us to get our minds off work for a bit, and relax with something we enjoy. But rather than just relaxing mindlessly, we might as well use that time to stretch our minds a bit.

Rather than just watching T.V., take the time to learn about the show you're watching. Learn about what went into creating the characters. Think about the worldview behind the show, and how it influences the way you view it. Think about the humor in it, and what makes it funny.

But don't take it too seriously. The point of a hobby is to relax. We need that time. So don't feel guilty if all you did was watch the show. Just don't let mindless entertainment become a significant part of your life. Let your entertainment help you become whole.

2. Take the time to talk.

One of the best ways to learn is to talk to the people around you. Take the time to have meaningful discussions. Don't be afraid to ask questions and posit ideas. Don't be afraid to be wrong.

The Christian life is the antithesis of the Lone Ranger mentality. The Christian life is meant to be lived in community.

One way I do this is through a conversation I have every other week. This conversation consists of me, my wife, and Ben — a great friend of mine. It's actually recorded, and turned into a podcast. But what is posted is not everything we talk about. Oftentimes, we talk for hours.

We talk about all kinds of stuff. We talk about our beliefs. We talk about current events and movies. But every time we talk I leave a better thinker. And I'm incredibly grateful for that.

Not only that, but I have a ton of fun with them as well. Our conversation is always the highlight of my week. We joke around, we pick on each other, but at the end of the day, we're challenged to think better.*

Outside of this group, I have individuals I trust that I go to with ideas and questions I have. People who think differently than I do. And I don't mean differently as in they're not Christian, although it's good to have people like that to talk to as well, but

---

* I encourage you to check out this podcast. Part of the reason we record this and post it is that we believe more people need to be able to have conversations like this. So see it as an example of what I'm talking about here. And in listening you might just be sharpened in your thinking, just like I am every week.

they go about things in a very different way than I do. Their thoughts are refreshing and, again, challenging.

One of these people is Rachel. Rachel is a person who sees the world in a very different way than I do. And she has a very sharp mind. When I have a thought I think needs some work, or a question I'm wrestling with, my wife and I will often go to lunch with her and hash it out. It's always great conversation.

There are others, but the last one I want to mention is my wife.

I have a wife who challenges me immensely. My wife is wicked smart, and she's smart in different areas than I am. We complement each other in our thinking. I'm more abstract and philosophical. She's more scientific. We have conversations about questions we're asking or things we're learning. And I'm constantly being refined because of our conversations.

So, to wrap this up, have some people who sharpen your mind. Get involved in conversations. Don't be afraid to disagree. And don't just have conversations with people who share your worldview, but venture out. Any time I get the chance to chat with someone who doesn't believe the way I do, I jump on it. It's always been a great experience.

3. Take the time to do.

Lastly, to make this happen — this life of intelligent faith — we need to take the time to do something.

For me, that's telling people about this message. It's writing, speaking, podcasting, blogging. For some, it's starting a business, a ministry, or making music. And still others, it's developing a great family.

Whatever it is you believe you're meant to do, take the time to act on it. Take the time to practice your craft.

To do this, it will require discipline, and scheduling, and long days. But if we, as Christians, want to change our culture, it will require us to do some work. It will require us to make the most of our time.

Wake up early, or stay up late. Just take the time to do something awesome.

The Christian life will, and should, take work. We are not, by nature, good. It is only Christ in us that makes us perfect before God. So the act of goodness in our lives will take effort. It will take study, reflection, and discipline. But it is done along with the power of the Holy Spirit. We are not alone, but we are accountable.

Epilogue

I know, it's almost over. Makes me sad too.

Don't be stupid.

"May God use me on the mission of Jesus as I am as wise as a serpent but as innocent as a dove. May God use my mind and my heart to bring the reason for the hope I have to others. And may God put others in my life who will ask for the hope as they watch me live it out."

Unknown

Writing the conclusion to a book is hard.

I feel like I need to inspire you. I feel like I need to say something that gets you to put into practice what you learned. But to be honest, I feel especially inadequate writing a conclusion. I'm typically not a very inspiring person. I make people think. I ask questions. I'm a teacher, not a preacher.

But I'll take a shot. And I'll keep it short. As you could probably tell, I'm a man of few words.

———————————————

We've learned a lot over the past hundred and something pages — at least I have. When getting to the end of writing this book, I had a lot of doubts.

Who am I to write a book? How do I know now is the right time? Aren't I going to learn more than what I know now? What if I mess this whole thing up? What if I'm doing it all wrong?

For me, this is the way life goes. I doubt. I question.

I'm a skeptic.

But after some thinking, and a pretty good pep talk from my wife, I realized that I'm never going to be perfect. And I'm never going to write a perfect book.

What I can do is write a decent book. One that may not sell a million copies and change the entire world, but might sell a couple hundred copies and change a single person's world.

If I must settle for that, so be it.

I'm not the only person who is like that. I'm a skeptic, but so are many others. I'm sure you know someone else who is the same way. It may even be you.

That's why you needed this book. That's why I needed to write it. Because those skeptics in your life and in our culture are looking for answers and they're looking for hope. Without smart Christians, they're unlikely to get it.

They need you.

They need you to live your life, and speak in a way that displays the beauty and truth of the Christian message.

That beauty, that truth, is wrapped up in the person of Christ. That, ultimately, is what our culture needs.

They need you to display Christ. And that's what all this is about.

It's about clearing away the stupid in the Christian image so our world can see Christ.

So please, don't be stupid.

Acknowledgements

My introverted personality often causes me to retreat from the people around me. I don't ask for help. I don't seek companions.

What I've learned, though, is God won't let me avoid them.

There are many people he has sent my way, who have shaped me, pushed me, and eventually helped make this book a reality.

I've had people like Dr. Jeff Voth, who has mentored me, and pushed me to go big and treat my dream like a reality. I've had Bobby Ross, who has been my creative pace setter. Just being in his presence makes me want to accomplish more. I've had Ben Kerr, my friend and podcast cohost, who always challenges me to think better. I've had my grandparents, a constant encouragement to continue in God's call on my life. And I've had my parents, who, from the beginning, have set a great example for what it means to lead a good life, and be diligent in what God calls you to.

And finally, I've had Sam. My wife, my social buffer, my editor, my constant dose of life, my encourager, and my friend.

Thank you, to all of you. (And so many more I couldn't fit in this book.) And thank God for you. As they say, I couldn't have done it without you.

Notes

1. C. S. Lewis, "Mere Christianity," in *The Complete C. S. Lewis Signature Classics* (New York: HarperOne, 2002), 116-17.

2. Cathy Lynn Grossman, "Young adults aren't sticking with church," *USA Today*, 2011, http://usatoday30.usatoday.com/printedition/life/20070807/d_churchdropout07.art.htm.

3. *The God Delusion Debate*, Richard Dawkins and John Lennox (Birmingham: Fixed Point Foundation, 2007), DVD.

4. drcraigvideos, "Dealing with Christian Doubt" *YouTube*. Online video clip, https://www.youtube.com/watch?v=wRm3PFFg97I.

5. Timothy Keller, *The Reason for God* (New York: Dutton, 2008), 187.

6. C. S. Lewis, *Perelandra* (New York: HarperCollins, 2012), 126, Kindle edition.

7. Jimmy Needham, "Forgiven and Loved," in *Not Without Love*, (Nashville: Inpop, 2008), iTunes.

8. C.S. Lewis, "They Asked For A Paper," in *Is Theology Poetry?* (London: Geoffrey Bless, 1962), 164-165.

9. Skye Jethani, "Video: Redefining Radical," *skyejethani.com*, September 24, 2014, https://skyejethani.com/video-redefining-radical/.

10. Walter Isaacson, *Steve Jobs* (New York: Simon and Schuster, 2011), 343.

11. Eric Metaxas, *Amazing Grace* (New York: HarperCollins, 2009), 58, Kindle edition.

12. ibid.

13. ibid.

14. Eric Metaxas, *Amazing Grace* (New York: HarperCollins, 2009), 85, Kindle edition.

15. Eric Metaxas, introduction to *Amazing Grace* (New York: HarperCollins, 2009), Kindle edition.

16. ibid.

17. Francis Shaeffer, (Address at the University of Notre Dame, April 1981), quoted in Nancey Pearcey, *Total Truth* (Wheaton: Crossway Books, 2008).

18. Eric Metaxas, introduction to *Amazing Grace* (New York: HarperCollins, 2009), Kindle edition.

19. "Eric Metaxas, *Amazing Grace* (New York: HarperCollins, 2009), 30, Kindle edition.

20. C. S. Lewis, "Christian Apologetics," in *God in the Dock: Essays on Theology and Ethics* (Grand Rapids: William B. Eerdman's Publishing Company, 1972), 93.

21. C. S. Lewis, "Sometimes Fairy Stories May Say Best What's to Be Said," in *On Stories: And Other Essays on Literature* (Boston: Houghton Mifflin Harcourt, 2002), Kindle edition.

22. C. S. Lewis, *The Voyage of the Dawn Treader* (New York: HarperTrophy, 2002), 269-70.

About the Author

Joshua Beck is a writer, podcaster, and teacher who lives in Oklahoma City, with his wife Sam. He writes at intelligo.in, is a host of the *Don't be stupid.* podcast, and teaches Apologetics and Ethics at a Christian high school. He has earned a B.A. in Theology and Philosophy, and is a little obsessed with both superheroes and C. S. Lewis.

To contact him, including invitations to speak, visit intelligo.in/contact. He would love to hear from you.

You can also find him on Twitter: @JoshuaBeck

Extras

Get more out of *Don't be stupid*.

30 Days to an Intelligent Faith

This is an email tutorial of sorts, that will help you put into action the ideas covered in the book. You'll get emails every other day for 30 days — because, let's be honest, nobody wants an email every day. You've already got enough of those to worry about.

So, 15 emails in total over a period of 30 days. They'll walk through how to pick a good book, the importance of community, liturgy and intelligent faith, and a whole lot more.

Don't be stupid. Resource Guide

This is a guide to resources that I think will help you better live out this life of intelligent faith. It will point you toward more than 50 books, podcasts, YouTube channels, websites, and apps that I absolutely love, and think will help you grow in your faith.

Don't be stupid. Discussion Guide

Whether you want to use it in a small group at your church, school, or with friends, the guide has questions for every chapter — to help facilitate deep discussion, and put into practice the things you've learned.

Find them all at: thedbsbook.com/extras

Intelligo

The home for thoughtful Christian commentary on faith, life, art, and culture.

Intelligo was founded by me. It's where most of my writing lives, and is the parent site to this book and the podcast. You'll find a steady stream of content, whether it be interviews, links to great posts  elsewhere on the web, or articles — from me and other great Christian writers — that will help you think through your faith and how it relates to life, art, and culture.

Find it at: intelligo.in

Don't be stupid.

The Podcast

Clever conversations on Christianity and culture

If you're looking for more after
reading *Don't be stupid.*, check
out the podcast. We dive deep
into the tough questions, and
have a ton of fun while doing
it. You'll learn a lot, and
probably laugh a lot too.

Find it at:
thedbspodcast.com

CPSIA information can be obtained
at www.ICGtesting.com
Printed in the USA
LVOW13s1829300118
564592LV00016B/1811/P